Holidays

Juneteenth

by R.J. Bailey

Bullfrog Books

Ideas for Parents and Teachers

Bullfrog Books let children practice reading informational text at the earliest reading levels. Repetition, familiar words, and photo labels support early readers.

Before Reading

- Discuss the cover photo. What does it tell them?

- Look at the picture glossary together. Read and discuss the words.

Read the Book

- "Walk" through the book and look at the photos. Let the child ask questions. Point out the photo labels.

- Read the book to the child, or have him or her read independently.

After Reading

- Prompt the child to think more. Ask: Does your family celebrate Juneteenth? What sorts of things do you see when it's Juneteenth?

Bullfrog Books are published by Jump!
5357 Penn Avenue South
Minneapolis, MN 55419
www.jumplibrary.com

Library of Congress Cataloging-in-Publication Data

Names: Bailey, R.J., author.
Title: Juneteenth / by R.J. Bailey.
Description: Minneapolis: Jump!, Inc., 2017.
Series: Holidays | Includes index.
Audience: Age 5–8. | Audience: Grade K to grade 3.
Identifiers: LCCN 2016005780 (print)
LCCN 2016006609 (ebook)
ISBN 9781620313534 (hard cover: alk. paper)
ISBN 9781624964008 (e-book)
Subjects: LCSH: Juneteenth—Juvenile literature.
Slaves—Emancipation—Texas—Juvenile literature.
African Americans—Anniversaries, etc.—Juvenile literature. | African Americans—Social life and customs—Juvenile literature. | Slaves—Emancipation—United States—Juvenile literature.
Classification: LCC E185.93.T4 B338 2017 (print)
LCC E185.93.T4 (ebook) | DDC 394.263—dc23
LC record available at http://lccn.loc.gov/2016005780

Editor: Kirsten Chang
Series Designer: Ellen Huber
Book Designer: Michelle Sonnek
Photo Researchers: Kirsten Chang & Michelle Sonnek

Photo Credits: All photos by Shutterstock except: Alamy, 6–7, 8, 23br; Getty, cover, 12–13, 22bl; iStock, 3, 16–17, 23bl; John G. Testa, 19, 22tl; SuperStock, 4, 10–11, 18, 20–21, 23tr; The Image Works, 14–15, 22tr.

Printed in the United States of America at Corporate Graphics in North Mankato, Minnesota.

Table of Contents

What Is Juneteenth?

Juneteenth is on June 19.

It is an African-American holiday.

On this day in 1865, slaves in Texas learned they were free.

They had a big celebration.

We celebrate, too.
How?

We go to church.
We give thanks.
We pray.

10

We go to a parade.

Look! It's Miss Juneteenth!

She waves at us.

People play music.
They dance.
They sing.

We have a cookout.
We eat BBQ. Yum!

BBQ

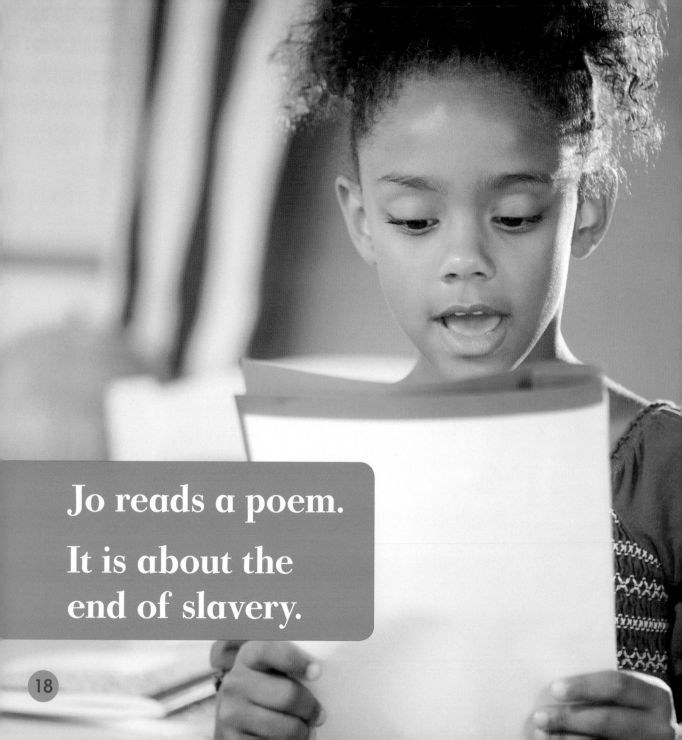

Jo reads a poem.

It is about the
end of slavery.

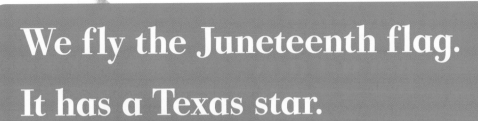

We fly the Juneteenth flag.

It has a Texas star.

Juneteenth is a special day!

Symbols of Juneteenth

flag

music

Miss Juneteenth

giving thanks

Picture Glossary

African-American
An American whose ancestors were born in Africa.

parade
An outdoor march that celebrates a special day or event.

BBQ
Food cooked outside over high heat; BBQ is short for barbecue.

slaves
People who are owned by other people and are forced to serve them.

23

Index

To Learn More

Learning more is as easy as 1, 2, 3.

1) Go to www.factsurfer.com

2) Enter "Juneteenth" into the search box.

3) Click the "Surf" button to see a list of websites.

With factsurfer.com, finding more information is just a click away.